My Favorite Spirituals

30 Songs for Voice and Piano

Arranged and Interpreted by
Roland Hayes

DOVER PUBLICATIONS
Garden City, New York

Bibliographical Note

This Dover edition, first published in 2001, is an unabridged republication of
*My Songs: Aframerican Religious Folk Songs Arranged and Interpreted by Roland
Hayes,* originally published as An Atlantic Monthly Press Book by Little, Brown
and Company, Boston.

International Standard Book Number

ISBN-13: 978-0-486-41701-1
ISBN-10: 0-486-41701-8

Manufactured in the United States of America
41701810   2021
www.doverpublications.com

TO

My beloved Wife and Daughter — Helen Alzada and Africa Fanzada —
whose love, understanding, and patient devotion
contributed so much to the creation of this book

AND TO

My friend, fellow artist, and great patron of music, Noel Sullivan,
on whose "Hollow Hills Farm," Carmel, California,
this book was prepared

Acknowledgment

Of my friend, Jacques Jolas, whose expert musical and literary observations helped me during the preparation of this book.

Of Laning Humphrey, whose knowledge of musical history afforded me valuable data.

Of the late Percival Parham, an enthusiastic accompanist and collaborator in the presentation of not only the Aframerican folk songs, but also the classics.

Of Miss Alice Freeman, for her tireless and capable efforts at copying and preparing *My Songs* for publication.

Foreword

I was born just twenty-four years after the Emancipation Proclamation. The atmosphere of the slave days was still strong at my place of birth and the religious folk songs of my people were being born out of religious experience at white heat. I have seen them being born in our religious services at the community Mount Zion Baptist Church at "Little Row" (now Curryville), Gordon County, Georgia. Here I heard great ritual sermons preached and prayers prayed, and I sang the Aframerican religious folk songs as a child with my parents and the church folk. Later, I was for four years a music special student at Fisk University in Nashville, Tennessee, and I acquired additions to the knowledge I already had of our folk songs from their pioneer collections.

In London and Paris, where I lived for twelve years, I made my home with some highly intelligent native Africans, mostly from the West Coast of Africa, who were taking university studies under government auspices. Discussions of the music of African peoples in Africa and Aframerican folk music were mutually enlightening. Aframerican folk songs forgotten since childhood sprang to my lips, and to my astonishment my native African audience joined in the music while expressing what they felt in their own language idiom. This pointed out to me the African characteristics in Aframerican folk songs, and in the heat of discovery the dross was separated from pure metal, to borrow a figure from the iron foundry in Chattanooga where I worked as a youth.

Eventually, I obtained recordings of African music, and a collection of musical instruments used in them, which I learned to manipulate well enough to understand them. From my African friends in London, and later from African visitors to my home, I learned how instrumental effects are sometimes implied in the vocal characteristics of the older Aframerican folk songs. These and other studies I have drawn upon in some of my accompaniments.

The term "Negro" is a misnomer when taken to mean that in anything but color the slaves within the borders of the various Southern states, or the various plantations — or even anywhere — were of one universal type. But for those Africans who were transplanted to the United States the term "Aframerican" seems fitting.

While compiling the thirty songs of this collection for general public interest, I have not by any means overlooked the solo performing artists who may wish to make one or more groups of songs for their concert or other programs. From each of the three panels of ten songs of this collection may be chosen two groups of four and more songs, well contrasted and diversified as to mood and key. For the church soloist who may wish to give an Easter program of Aframerican songs, I direct attention to the third panel of ten songs that deal with the Life of Christ. There you will find "Passion Music" specially arranged with instrumental prelude and connecting interludes so that a continuous performance (from the "Last Supper" through the "Ascension") may be given without a break in the music, if you choose to do so.

ROLAND HAYES

BROOKLINE, MASSACHUSETTS
February 17, 1948

Contents

Panel One
EVENTS OF THE OLD TESTAMENT

Panel Two
ABSTRACTIONS FROM THE TEACHINGS OF BOTH OLD AND NEW TESTAMENTS

Panel Three
THE LIFE OF CHRIST

Christ's Birth, Boyhood and Ministry

The Passion of Our Lord

My Favorite Spirituals

My Songs

The Africans captured for the southern plantations brought with them from many parts of Africa, with their various cultures, a skill and creative power. Being creators, these transplanted Africans fused their American experiences and their native gifts and produced a new art — the Aframerican religious folk song, the "spiritual."

The conscious and subconscious experiences of the Aframerican are the core of this collection of songs. They share basic human qualities with songs of many peoples, regardless of race, creed or color; and speak of that endless search for better understanding of the Divine Law which shapes the destinies of men; that something which is inherent in all great works of art.

Much of my life has been spent in re-creating the inspiration which poets and musicians have breathed into the songs of many peoples that more and more may come to feel the inspirational qualities in them and derive lasting benefit therefrom. That is what I am trying to do with the songs of my own people.

Africa speaks to the world of art in this music. Just as I myself, the music was born a child of American slaves, but it is the inheritor of a true culture peculiar to Africa.

They are, of course, the songs of no one person, yet the experiences from which they have sprung have been so much a part of my life that the songs have become a part of me. In that sense they are My Songs.

Thomas Jefferson, who was a violinist and well versed in music, wrote in 1782:

> In music the blacks are generally more gifted than the whites, with accurate ears for tune and time; and they have been found capable of imagining a small catch.[1]

This was probably the first published analysis on the subject of music of the African slave.

Probably the next oldest observation was made in the 1830's by the brilliant Fanny Kemble, who wrote a journal of her experiences on the rice plantations of her American husband, Pierce Butler, near Darien, Georgia. Writing about two young Aframericans who rowed her in a boat, she said, "Rowing yesterday evening through a beautiful sunset into a more beautiful sunrise, my two sable boatmen entertained themselves and me with alternate strophe and antistrophe of poetical description of my personal attractions."[2]

Here we have two solo voices, singing antiphonally — to improvised words, if not also improvised music. Alternation of solo and chorus is a universal African procedure, and is the basic pattern of the Aframerican folk song, and there is in both cases a considerable latitude in its application. At times, both in African music and in Aframerican folk songs, the chorus is so reduced as to leave practically a solo, with only occasional choral punctuation. Vocal solos with no choral addition, however, are by no means unknown to Africa or to Aframerica. There are many such solo-type songs amongst our Aframerican folk songs.

Claims have been advanced in recent years that Aframerican religious folk songs originated purely and simply in the slaves' imitation of their white masters' hymns. Elsewhere in this book I speak of the Aframerican having "fused his American experiences and his native gifts and produced a new art — the Aframerican religious folk song (the so-called 'spiritual')." If this is what is meant by the said advocators' "imitation" claim, I shall be quiet. It is a fact that the Aframerican, as do other folk, often blends related

---

[1] *Notes on Virginia.* A catch is a kind of round, a canon in which two or more singers perform a part alternately. As only one part was written out, each succeeding singer had to catch his part. The first printed collection of catches is of the year 1609.

[2] *Journal of a Residence on a Georgian Plantation, 1838–1839.* Harper & Brothers, 1863.

items of meaning with his own, which he finds in other peoples and things, but it certainly is not his practice, generally, to throw away many of his original possessions.

I do not feel it to be incongruous to harmonize Aframerican religious folk songs. It is a common fallacy to generalize that these folk songs are definitely unisonal. Time and again very definite harmony may be found included in the melodies themselves. The rise and fall of a melody can be seen in the opening phrase in "Deep River":

Here we have the chord in successive notes, rather than simultaneously, of G, E♭, C, on the descending slur of D–E–E–P R–I–V–E–R. Then we follow the course of this to the point, *My home is over Jordan.* Between *is* and *o–ver* is a full octave.

I learned through observation that fundamentally the African and Aframerican folk songs had these things in common: rhythmic idiom and, above all, verse and refrain. However, there is the striking difference of language. Also, I observed that the Aframerican, having embraced and absorbed much of Western education, custom and manner, speaks over more extended phrases in his singing than the average African native has the habit of doing.

Further observation revealed that though the African and Aframerican song and dance forms are more or less identical, their manner and method of handling the rhythmic pulse and syncopation differed much. The African natives with whom I came in contact conceived of their rhythm as a main pulse beat of one count to the measure. They divide and subdivide all of the (sometimes) great variety of rhythmic material they maneuver between the pulse points. The big Mother Drum — as they call it — carries the main pulse beat while the variations are distributed between other instruments which strike in, after the pulse beat, anywhere from one sixty-fourth part of the rhythmic meter count to one sixty-fourth part of the count before the next pulse beat. These (in-between) variation rhythmic patterns frequently take the form of triplets which, as they compound within the rhythmic count of ONE, accomplish wonders in the sense of harmonic variety.

But the Aframerican realizes his rhythm quite differently. His meter is TWO–FOUR or FOUR–FOUR counts to the measure. This gives a rather square feeling form to his rhythmic pattern; and a certain rigidity. As a consequence, even a slight variance in the meter is apt to throw him out of his rhythmic balance. On the contrary, the African, because he fixes his rhythms flexibly at the pulse point of ONE, can pick himself up, at will, on any divisional spot or variation within the rhythmic phrase.

The native African seems to build his *crescendi* in the process of compound rhythm, while the Aframerican arrives at his by *pounding*, exaggeratedly, on his rhythmic beats of TWO–FOUR or FOUR–FOUR to the measure.

Despite the great difference which the Aframericans' embrace of Western fashion makes, however, there are still to be found fragmentary folk song items here in the United States which savor of pure native African origin. For the sake of example, I here present four "catch" ditties of Aframerican and African design which I invite the reader to compare. The first, "Lit'l Girl, Lit'l Girl!" is a small Aframerican catch; the second, a West African catch with phonetic text ("Di ai dia"); the third, an Aframerican religious folk song; and the fourth a northern Nigerian or West African catch ("Adika!"):

1

2

3

4

A - di - ka,— A - di - ka!

Té - ri in-a - ga, Té - ri A-di-ka! Té-ri in-a - ga, Té-ri A-di-ka!—

Not infrequently I am asked, "Should Negro spirituals be sung in the crude, broad dialect which we hear spoken as well as sung by members of your race?" In answering this question, I should like to point to factors having direct bearing on the subject. It must be remembered that my people sprang originally from many and varied tribal areas in Africa as well as from many different American regions. Hence, types, customs, manners and practices differ accordingly. What one individual may employ as dialect in his or her mode of pronunciation generally differs from that of another — even in the same locality. There are, on the other hand, those few among the many of us whom I should call singing poets in dialect.

These high priests of folk song utterance are very discriminating in their taste, choice and use of dialect. They are those who have developed an extraordinary skill at making dialect word forms coalesce with the thought to be expressed. The actual sound as well as the blending of the words as used by them is quite different from the feeling conveyed by the same words seen in cold print.

First, I would say that no one should attempt to use dialect in singing the songs of my people who has not, beforehand, thoroughly mastered the idiom of our mastersingers and the dialect itself. To my way of thinking, rightness or wrongness in the use of dialect depends much more on the individual, and the use he would make of it, than upon the dialect itself.

Then I, particularly, wish to emphasize that *all* of the so-called traditional Negro habits in the singing of his songs should be gone over in detail. At the risk of being labeled a purist, I see current overexaggerations as vulgarities and malefactions. They are superficial parodies, because they simply fail to reach the profound religious expression which is the very heartbeat of the Aframerican religious folk song.

Whether or not the singing of the folk songs of my people is effective depends upon the proper approach of the individual or group who sings them. This proper approach cannot be attained by a superficial survey. First, one must realize that the inner significance of these songs stems from a universal human source, common to all mankind. The next step is to know the Aframerican song design through an understanding of what the Aframerican's life situation is as against that of other individual races. A given dialect word form can look ever so raw in print, and yet when the meaning welling up through the word form is properly caught and has its way with the singer, there is an immediate transformation. What before might have appeared uncomely in the performer quite amazingly becomes agreeable. I am certain that my reader has experienced the truth of what I have just related, even as I have.

Above all, I would remind any performer that that which fills, and ofttimes overflows, the choicest of Aframerican folk song utterance (and all singing for that matter) is implicit in those most important of items called "Right Spirit of Song" and "Meaning in the Words." These phenomena, when invited, maintain a position in our conscious feeling and make projective agencies of every fiber. Therefore, self-abnegation and complete subjection of the ego are demanded of all who would sing.

What takes place in the heart of the performer, unconsciously often, escapes the average listener whose rapt attention is engaged with the sensuous pleasure of listening. I am convinced of that, particularly, in the singing of spirituals by members of my own race. My eighty-three-year-old friend, William L. Shelton, carries in himself his African heritage. His mastery in the effective, effortless use of dialect, his sounds so deep and rich, with a twinkle in his voice, all have overtones. They speak to me clearly, echoing the dim past — our ancient African ancestry and tribal memories. There is no sign of his great age in his tall, erect figure, except in a slight stoop that makes him carry his head the merest bit at an angle as if listening eagerly. His brown eyes can lighten with an astonishing glow that is like the sun darting suddenly amid the shadows of a forest. Gravely courteous as he is, you feel a communion of warmth in his rugged person that strikes you as singularly elemental. It points straight through underbrush and bramble to a single item of inner strength and unity of soul.

I have wept because I was unable to duplicate in my voice that which he gives to his, to reach out toward my African ancestry in search of that fundamental unsophisticated power, infinite, unmistakable, in the cadence of his voice. Not within the range of my experience, since listening to Charles Foster, the great Aframerican preacher and most gifted of singing minstrels, and a forester, Will Garlington (both of my childhood memory), have I heard such soul-stirring qualities in a human voice. From their mysterious source, verities long lost to the consciousness of mankind seemed unveiled. These verities, shrouded in time and antiquity. become living realities, as if these men carried within them the unbroken line of human destiny from days when men walked with God.

The persistent upsurge of the speech and thought of their remote ancestors grips many Aframericans inwardly in their thought and often in their speech — whether they be deficient in education and culture or the reverse. Many Aframericans, also, have the characteristic habit of including enclitic vowel sounds in their use of the English language, as if it lacked potency of expression. In many of the songs of this collection, for example, will be found enclitic vowels sandwiched in between English words. For instance, the song title "In That Morning" expressed in Aframerican dialect is "In-a-Dat Mornin'." Another example is that of the song text "Give Way, Jordan," which in Aframerican dialect is "Give-a Way, Jordan." There is more than one reason why certain Aframericans habitually give themselves to this practice. When my people wish to express something of marked characterization over other words, they want the terms they use to be so substantial, in every part, as to win immediate favorable reaction. If they feel that to include an enclitic expression in their utterance will accomplish their purposes, they lose no time in putting it to work. We must not overlook that very significant reason of atavistic clinging to certain items of our dialect as part of the language of our original ancestors. This language of our original ancestors must have possessed such high-frequency vibration that it became an effective medium of communication between Nature, God and themselves.

There is wonder for many of us even in the sound of dialect terms that embrace certain constellating letter combinations. This type of dialect term occurs frequently in the songs of my people. An example of interest in this connection may be experienced in "Dry Bones" — a song of this collection. In the sentence, "They are going to walk around," the Aframerican originator expressed

10

the same thought in dialect as "Dey gona wauk aroun'." The significant high-frequency vibration in words like "gona" reminds me of an experience I had very recently, when a learned native African lady visited my home. This African personage knew the English language very well, and she spoke it well, too, though I noticed that certain characteristics of her mother tongue were evident. When she spoke such words as "around" and "going," the sounds were "arounh" and "gonh." The vowels *o* and *ou* were given by her with great purity of sound and in rich, sonorous cadences. She seemed fairly to caress the sounds she made on these two vowels. I felt a profound nostalgia as I listened to her vocal utterances — utterances which mirrored and conveyed a meaning far beyond the literal sense of the words she spoke.

This collection is a brief anthology of what I prefer to call Aframerican, rather than "American Negro," religious folk songs. It is made up of three smaller anthologies. One group describes events in the Old Testament, another deals with those in the New Testament. Between these is a group which I call abstractions from both the Old and the New Testament, based upon the teachings of the Bible more than on episodes from it.

By following this plan, I hope to make clear the creative power of the Aframerican musician in the realm of narration, imaginative religious thinking and musical expression.

Above all, however, my object is to have this book considered on the plane of Aframerican musical art. I believe that the second half of the New Testament group of songs is worthy of a place beside early European composers' efforts at depiction of the Passion of Our Lord.

There are obvious difficulties in carrying out my aims. For practical reasons, solo voice and piano must suffice to represent folk songs originally sung by an unaccompanied chorus. But similar difficulties preceded such collections as Weckerlin's *Echoés du Temps Passé*, making madrigals available for performance by one voice and the piano. The solution in both cases must be a synthesis aiming at a generally correct impression of the character and historical atmosphere of the original. Again for practical reasons, it has been necessary to try to reconcile to the conventions of European musical notation a number of usages which the African musician developed without that system. In fact, had he known of the system, he probably would have scoffed at it as inadequate for his needs.

In the songs of this collection will be seen the dialect word "de" which many Aframericans use instead of "the." The rule for the correct phonetic sound of "de" is the same as that in the English language. When "de" precedes a word that begins with a vowel, the letter *e* has the same sound as *e* in "be." When "de" precedes a word that begins with a consonant, the *e* has the same sound as *u* in "uh."

Art forms and Aframerican folk songs do meet on the common ground of purpose, feeling and fitting form. All three are amply demonstrated in *My Songs*.

The religious songs of my people are considered outside the historic evolution of music as characterized by the works of such masters as, for example, the great Venetian composer Giovanni Gabrielli (1557–1612), and Heinrich Schutz (1585–1672). Nor can the question of such forms as motets or cantatas have any serious bearing on the subject. But the incomparable freedom of the speech of Bach in "Saint Matthew Passion," and his musical poetic style, at times find their counterpart in the religious spirit of the artless outpourings of a musical race.

A famous teacher and scholar of Vienna to whom I had come to seek guidance in the mastery of Bach's style convinced me of that. I vividly remember his astonishment on hearing me sing some Aframerican folk songs; an astonishment caused by the spiritual affinity of my songs with the spirit and style of the great German master. "But you have it all there," he assured me; "it is the same language."

I believe it can be said that the Aframerican, without benefit of the tradition of his white brothers, created from within his own soul and intelligence. Drawing on his reservoir of musical instinct, embracing Old and New Testaments with the tenacity of a plant, he sank his roots deep down into its Truth, bringing both Old and New Testaments into close relationship with himself with utter naturalness and proper perspective.

The Biblical stories in this collection have been used in modern times. The English, for example, incorporated them in the miracle plays of the fifteenth century and Milton used the Samson story in *Samson Agonistes*. In our own day, Thomas Mann has expanded the Joseph story in a many-volumed work. The Aframerican has used the same material with a difference. It is of that difference that I have first to speak.

12

"In the Beginning was the Word." The roots of the songs of my people penetrate deep into the significance of the "Word." "The Word was God!" Indeed the Bible is the foundation, the cornerstone, as 'twere, of all that the Aframerican has revealed and projected through the means of his religious folk songs. The Bible is the source, and any interpretation deviating from this fact is the grossest of errors.

My people found in the grandeur of the Biblical word and poetry a fountain of illimitable solace. From out the horizon of their tragic lot rose a sublime illumination; an all-stimulating ray of hope for deliverance through the Star of Bethlehem. Its radiance fostered a faith in its promise that drew inspiration in endless play of imagination around the revelations of the Bible. This enduring Faith moved with complete confidence amid its allegories, symbols and parables. Word and music became one; the religious ecstasy as well as sheer intoxication with the sound of the Word itself flowing forth into exciting expansions of religious experience.

A thing of major importance, the African's love of allegory (in the U.S.A.), enabled him to substitute himself, his present condition and future hope, for Semitic Bible personages and situations.

The texts of these Aframerican religious folk songs are a blend of versified religious paraphrases and amplifying remarks of the poets. Also, this collection should afford some notion of the comprehensiveness of the oral Bible. On some plantations slaves were allowed to go occasionally to a church set aside or sanctioned by the masters for them, over which a white clergyman would preside. On intermediate Sundays the slaves would assemble in the cabin of one of their own pious fellow men, who, heaven knows how, had obtained some little knowledge of reading. In my own mother's case, it was by means of her exchange of cookies for a daily report from her master's children on what they had learned that day.

PANEL ONE
Events of the Old Testament

I. I'll Make Me a Man

(Genesis I.26)

Just as the late James Weldon Johnson, the Aframerican poet, heard some of the mastersinging ministers of my people in his childhood in Florida, so it was my childhood experience in my "Angel Mo" community in Georgia to hear the same sermons sung-preached by Charles Foster and others. These great song sermons and prayers, too, of the mighty Aframerican preachers of pre-Civil War days became Ritual and thereafter were given by all the great and near-great who followed.

The particular song sermon, "I'll Make Me a Man," which is the first song of this collection, is an excerpt from the "Creation" sermon. Mr. Johnson's collection of poems called *God's Trombones* contains the words of this sermon in its entirety.

When I recall the mastersinger types, the original creator of the song sermon, "Creation," stands vividly before me, a giant in stature, commanding in presence and eloquent in delivery. Yes, I see him in magnificent, dynamic gesture fired by the Divine Spirit as he strides (even prances) over the pulpit platform with the Holy Bible on his shoulder, depicting the manner of God's creative methods in these thunderously eloquent tones: *"Then God walked around."* In these words are majesty, and the sonorous simplicity of utterance such as to stir the imagination. This great master of oratory, as with the plastic strokes of a sculptor, carved out sentence upon sentence which seemed to pause in their cosmic flight to embrace a loving image tenderly, *"Like a mammy bending over her babe."*

"And man became a living soul." With these words, given as with a hammer stroke in a stirring outburst of eloquence, ends this truly great song sermon. It was born of masterful imagery of a heaven-taught soul — but otherwise untutored. The music in this song realizes its mood in a setting spare and tense which alternates between chant and dramatic recitation; where all is bound together by an inevitable rhythmic pulse that rises to an emotional climax with the reiterated, exultant *"Amen."*

I'll Make Me a Man

Declamando

sat down ___ on the side of a hill, God sat ___ down where He could think, God

sat down ___ by a deep, wide riv - er, God sat ___ down with His head in His hands, God

thought and thought, till He ___ thought "I'll ___ make me a man."___

Up from the bed ___ of ___ the riv - er, ___ God ___ scooped-a the

18

clay._____ And by the bank of the__ riv - er,__ God__ kneeled Him

down. And there_____ this great God al - - might y!__

Who lit__ the sun and fixed it in the sky, Who flung the stars__ to the__ most far

cor-ners of the night, Who round-ed the earth in__ the hol-low of His hand, this

19

great God, This great God like a mam-my bend-ing o-ver her babe,

kneeled down in the dust, toil-ing o - ver this-a lump of clay till He

shaped it, He shaped it, till He shaped it in His own im - age. Then

in - to it He blew the breath of life, And man be-came a liv-ing soul.

II. Let My People Go!

(*Exodus VIII.1*)

Exodus VIII.1 is clearly an evocation that mirrors the lot of my race as a people. It cannot be said too often that behind the heartbreaking beauty of human fate stands in undiminishing, stark reality the story of man's injustice and cruelty to his fellow man, as an accusing, moral reminder toward a better way of life. As Moses opens his soul to the presence of God, so we experience in this song a mutation, a melting over of ourselves through Moses to God. There is grave simplicity in the lines of this noble song that has stamped it indelibly with universal human appeal. When France was in the grip of the Nazis, its poets and artists of the underground sought expression through the symbol of the word. There is evidence of this kind of camouflage in "Let My People Go." Not daring to speak openly of freedom, my people, enslaved, found through song a means to give this utterance of incredible strength.

Let My People Go!

Arranged by Roland Hayes

Op - pressed so hard they could not stand,
"If not I'll strike your first born dead!"

Let my peo-ple go.
Let my peo-ple go.

Go down Mo-ses

rubato cresc. a tempo

way down in Eg-ypt's land. Tell old Pha-roah to

lento

1.
let my peo-ple go.

D.S.

2.
let my peo-ple go.

1. espressivo

a tempo

D.S.

2.

23

III. Deep River

(Joshua III.8)

At the source of this tune ring the words from Joshua: "When ye are come to the brink of the water of Jordan, ye shall stand still in Jordan."

It is primitive in its wonder; yes, ecstasy before the incredible. "As God was with Moses, so shall I be with him at the time of my delivery." In the embrace of death lies fulfillment. As celebrated as the theme of Beethoven's Fifth, the musical phrase, *"Deep river, my home is over Jordan,"* lies deeply rooted in the consciousness of mankind. It has a suggestive quality of inescapable power. Three times the last phrase, *"I want to cross over into camp ground,"* is repeated. That repetition, a sort of incantation, is not unlike the litanies of the Catholic Church. Repetitions are phenomena of imaginative, poetic intoxication that, choosing word sounds irrespective of meaning, identifies the person with the mood. Thus I remember Will Garlington felling a tree and chanting a monotony of syllables, transforming the felling of the tree, and himself, into an entity.

Deep River

Arranged by Roland Hayes

want to cross o - ver in - to camp-ground. O don't you want to go_ to that

gos - pel feast, To that prom - ised land, where all is peace. Lord, I

want to cross o - ver in - to camp-ground, Lord, I want to cross o - ver in - to

camp - ground,_ Lord, I want to cross o - ver in - to camp-ground.

IV. Ezekiel Saw de Wheel

(*Ezekiel I.21–23*)

There is a kind of humor, a quality of smile that can accompany serious matter, either as a natural balance to gravity or as the more elusive spirit of radiance. Often, in the songs of my people, a light humor, not lacking in serious import, however, can enter very aptly and deftly into reverence. We have a way of standing on both feet and, though we lose ourselves in the contemplation of our spiritual destiny as in the preceding songs, we are children of the earth. The earthiness enables us to give voice to our dialogue with God in the manner, at times, of the cajoling child. We surround God on all sides. So our rhythms and metaphors dance before God. With a child's delight at glimpsing a toy, we lift, temporarily, the realism of an object out of the context of a poem and it lights with sunny frivolity. "Ezekiel Saw de Wheel" sings of the oneness of the human family — *"De big wheel run by faith; an' de lit'l wheel run-a by de grace of God."* The power of the symbol, the profundity of the experience, are barely hidden under the saving grace of light. The big wheel — there springs to mind a big wheel in a circus — motion, gaiety, wonder, spontaneous humor.

Ezekiel Saw de Wheel

Arranged by Roland Hayes

ze-kiel saw de wheel of time, Ev-'ry spoke was of hu-man kind, A

wheel in a wheel, Way in de mid-dle of de air. O de

col canto

big wheel run by faith, An' de lit-'l wheel run-a by de grace of God, A

mf   *mp*   *p*

wheel in a wheel, Way in de mid-dle of de air.

col canto

V. Lit'l David Play on Your Harp

(*Psalms CXXXVII.4*)

"Lit'l David play on yo' harp." How deeply the accents of this most beautiful among the Psalms must have haunted the first singer, "Little David." *"How can we sing the Lord's songs in a strange land?"* Was it like an echo of his own people's anguish finding constancy in song and word? I recall years ago, when with the unpredictable waywardness of artistic consciousness this song came back to me. On a muleback ride-walk over fields and up the slopes of Granada, in Spain's Sierra Nevadas, and thinking of Schubert's "Der Musenssohn," I suddenly heard the tones of a flute, played by a peasant coming across the hills. With that single sound, so full of pathos, there flashed through me the sunny tenderness of "Lit'l David," with a definite clarity of its meaning and feeling.

Lit'l David Play on Your Harp

Arranged by Roland Hayes

piece." Da - vid said to me, "How can I play, when I'm

in a strange land?" Da - vid, play on yo' harp, Hal - le -

lu, Hal - le - lu-jah, Lit - 'l Da - vid play on yo' harp, Hal - le -

lu. Da - vid play on yo' harp, Hal - le - lu, Hal - le -

lu - jah, Lit - 'l Da - vid play on yo' harp, Hal - le - lu!

VI. Dry Bones

(*Ezekiel XXXVII.1–15*)

This song deals with the resurrection of my people. Its hope, like that of Israel, is revived in living with the promise of Christ's Kingdom. "I will set my sanctuary in the midst of them forevermore."

In the form of an exhortation, this ringing narrative chooses as always the most vivid means to appeal dramatically through the emotions. By similar means the Biblical oratorios react on us, and indeed the opening recitative suggests the spaciousness of a Handel recitative.

Elsewhere in this collection we have texts drawn from Biblical chapters far more simple to follow than the complexities of Ezekiel. Here in his delivery of the sermon on the "dry bones" is an example of how the gifted Aframerican preacher adapted himself to the limitations of his congregation. To heighten the effect and to ease the way to the understanding of his flock, he impersonates the questioning layman in his congregation. *"Tell me, how did de bones get together wid de leg bone?"* He poses the query with such fervor that the whole of his congregation assumes the attitude of the imaginary questioner — while his tones hint before the unfolding of the miracle.

The mode interchanges between major and minor. The narrative of his discourse is told in repeated phrases, bit by bit — a voice from the congregation interrupting at intervals — while his listeners, with wonder and eagerness, wait to hear the prophecy fulfilled.

Dry Bones

Arranged by Roland Hayes

com - mand-ed de bones to rise.___ Dey gon - na

walk a - roun'. Dry bones, dey gon - na walk a - roun'___ wid de

Dry bones, dey gon - na walk a - roun'. Dry bones, why don't you

rise an' hear de word of de Lord.___ "Tell me,

how____ did de bones ____ get to - geth - er wid de leg

bone? ____ Pro - - phe - - sy!"

ad lib.

"Ah, well, de toe bone con - nect - ed wid de

foot bone; De foot bone con - nect - ed wid de

an - kle bone; De an - kle bone con - nect - ed wid de

leg bone; De leg bone con - nect - ed wid de

knee bone; De knee bone con - nect - ed wid de thigh

bone. Rise and hear de word of de Lord!

D.S.

VII. Give-a Way, Jordan

(*Joshua III*)

For me there lies in this melody the poignancy of something far away, ancestral. In the symbol of River Jordan lies promise of magic fulfillment. Through it, through the flow of music and word, sings the meekness and humility of the soul crossing over to the Throne of God. The reference to Nebuchadnezzar seems sudden and irrelevant. But no doubt this fragment from the Book of Daniel had its own poetic logic for the first singer.

Give-a Way, Jordan

Arranged by Roland Hayes

39

saw ___ the three He - brew chil - lun boun' hands an' feet. ___ I

mus' go for to see my Lord. ___ Give-a way, ___

Jor - dan, Give-a way, ___ Jor - dan, Lord, ___

Give-a way, ___ Jor - dan, I mus' go for to see my Lord.

40

VIII. Two Wings

(Ezekiel I.2, 5, 6)

Again we find, in "Two Wings," evidence of detachment of humor that achieves a freedom. It is a priceless heritage in my people's fantasy to set free serious concern — life, death, union with God — through the ability to laugh, to smile, to follow gaily in the steps of poetic suggestion. A particular charm of this song lies in its syncopation, which must be sung without stress or heavy accent, on tiptoe, so to speak. The motion of the melody is like reaching for something not quite within reach. With the accompaniment played in strict time, but with elasticity here and there, the airy quality of the voice part will be realized. To escape the triviality which a too thumpy accent might give to this beautiful song, it is well to remember the sheer ecstasy of mystic longing that trembles in word and music. To me, the song represents a metamorphosis clearly taken from Ezekiel, Chapter I, verses 2, 5, 6. The more ardent, slower middle part of the song achieves a synthesis of Old and New Testament promise and fulfillment.

Two Wings

Arranged by Roland Hayes

44

IX. Didn't My Lord Deliver Daniel?

(*Daniel VI*)

"Didn't My Lord Deliver Daniel?" corroborates what is said in my remarks on "Give-a Way, Jordan." The soul about to cross over recalls the promise to Joshua in the Old Testament. The music is built on a pentatonic scale and has, despite its apparent hopeful character, a strange feeling of poignant longing.

Didn't My Lord Deliver Daniel?

Arranged by Roland Hayes

why not - a ev - er - y man?_____ He__ de - liv - ered__ Dan - iel from de

li - on's__ den, An'__ Jo - nah from de bel - ly of de whale. An' de

He - brew chil - lun from de fi - er - y fur - nace, An' a why not__ de - liv - er po'__

1.   D.S. 2.
me?_____ A - did - n't   me?_____

X. A Witness

(The Sum of Many Prophets)

In characteristic and picturesque pattern, the narrator in "A Witness" summons prophets of both Old and New Testaments. Knitting them together, he presents to his congregation the oneness of Truth. He concludes the song sermon with the pertinent question: *"Who'll be a witness for my Lord?"* This song sermon, like "Dry Bones" and "I'll Make Me a Man," seems to me to be based on sound principles of psychology and aesthetics. Audience participation, rapt attention in the art of worship by means of word and music, has been pointed out to me by religious leaders as of significant importance. The need for such identification with religious feeling is greatly felt. Perhaps the ecstasy, the forgetting of one's self in a communal feeling of faith, trust and love, contains a hint for both music and religion. In these simple, naïve, religious song poems may live the germ for some future art form, which as with Bach and the chorale will achieve its typical, grandiose expression. In their very simplicity, these song sermons speak, profoundly, to whoever hears them with simplicity of heart and reverence for their spiritual and human truths.

A Witness

Arranged by Roland Hayes

God cre-a - ted him out-a de dust, Then God made a wom-an, an' He call'd her_ Eve, An'

told her not to eat of the for-bid-den tree. Now that's the fust wit-ness for my Lord, That's

the fust wit - ness for my Lord. You

read a - gain, an' you'll un-der-stan', Me-thus-a-lah was the old-est man. He

48

lived nine hun-dred an'-a six-ty_ nine; He died an'went to Heav'n,Lord, in due time. Me-

thus'-lah was a wit-ness for my_ Lord; Me-thus'-lah was a wit-ness for my_ Lord.

You read a-bout Sam-son from his_ birth; He

was the strong-est_ man on_ earth. Sam-son went out_ at-a one time, An'

killed a thou-sand of de Phil-is - tine. De - li-lah fooled Sam-son, this we_ know, For the

Ho - ly Bi - ble tells us_ so._ She shaved his head_ just as clean as your hand, An' his

strength be-came as_ a com-mon man. Now that's an-oth-er wit-ness for my_ Lord, Now_

that's an-oth-er wit - ness for my_ Lord.

Dan-iel__ was a He-brew chile, Who went to pray to his God for a while. The

Largo

king at__ once for__ Dan-iel did send, An'__ he put him down in de li-ons' den. De

Lord sent an an - gel,__ de li - ons for to keep. Then

Dan - iel laid down,__ An' he went to sleep. Dan -

iel was a wit-ness Dan - iel was a wit - ness Then

(For my Lord) (For my Lord)

a tempo

who'll be a wit-ness? Now who'll be a wit-ness? Who'll

(For my Lord) (For my Lord)

_____ be a wit-ness? Oh, who'll ____ be a

(For my Lord)

cresc. *f* *f*

wit - ness ___ for my ___ Lord? _____

PANEL TWO
Abstractions from the Teachings of Both Old and New Testaments

Abstractions from the Teachings of Both Old and New Testaments

African songs give instruction — often by allegory — and improvised song deals with a topical episode or emotion.

The Aframerican religious folk songs are belatedly discovered to be emblematic not of weakness and degradation under slavery, but of power which carried the race through slavery. The enslaved Indian of early Spanish conquest perished. The Aframerican slave survived.

As a race (the history of one hundred and fifty years of slavery in his consciousness) the Aframerican could easily have disintegrated, losing self-respect, initiative, hope. There was divine purpose in his singing. Balancing himself on the deep springs of his musical nature gave him flexibility, fluidity, hence continuity. His religion, his song, became a working principle; the promise had to be all around him. In work and church and field, song and word became functional, integrated. He could laugh at himself and others. My own mother, in the twinkle of an eye, could illumine a subject sacred to her with a shaft of golden humor. Also, there were the workers in the field discussing the Sunday gathering and song festival amid peals of laughter and discriminating review. This attitude, which springs from many sources, has helped shape the astonishing growth of the Aframerican intellectually and musically. Not the least of these sources I see in the many facets of his musical nature, that turns his inner eye, as in these songs, to God and man with purpose, feeling and form.

Giving to the appearance of things their true reality, achieving a philosophy of eminent good sense, has often mistakenly been labeled "happy-go-lucky." But it seems to me to be a kind of wisdom, born out of experience and sense of proportion. This faculty represents uncanny and remarkable resourcefulness, besides furnishing proof of a psychological truth.

It was brought home to me in handsome terms one day down in Georgia. The community of Angel Mo' Farm and I had planned a special festive event, featuring barbecue and baseball games. For two days there was vigorous preparation putting the ground in shape for the big day; when at the end of the second day I announced to the group of eight men my intention to have a look around, there didn't seem to be any particular enthusiasm for my inquisitiveness. They just draped themselves around their tools to await my verdict with rugged calm. On being informed that, according to my judgment, much was still to be done, they simply walked away. Feeling just a bit foolish, I had a creeping suspicion of having been put in my place. My foreman, sensing the tense moment and my chagrin, sprang to the rescue. "Mr. Hayes," he said, "I know what you want and you ought to have it, but if you make it too fine, we won't enjoy ourselves. You see, Mr. Hayes, what it takes to have a good time for us is in us, and we can have a good time on a rock pile."

I think there is more to this story than meets the eye. There are toughness, self-sufficiency and good common sense.

This group of eight men represented as many more important members of a singing choir in our Angel Mo' Farm community. Competitive singing by various community choirs, scattered over an area of thirty to fifty miles, afforded a great incentive for our community folk to get together once or twice a week for rehearsals. On such Sundays as they were to go abroad to sing in other communities, the singers would pile into trucks, wagons pulled by mules, or any other possible conveyance and, rejoicing, would be heard singing snatches of favorite song passages as they journeyed along. These community folk had loads of fun; good fun, which their Bible teachings helped to keep chaste and in proper proportion.

It was my habit — especially in the early part of my return home after thirty years' absence — to give concerts in the community area. The proceeds from these concerts went toward some community welfare. This gesture of good will was much appreciated by my homefolks, who in turn wished to do something for me. So it was that one night in the winter of 1930, the Angel Mo' community singers announced to me that they were going to give me an evening of music in my own Angel Mo' farmhouse. The night came and my home was fittingly prepared for the occasion. Great waves of heat poured forth from wood fires which had been lit in the four fireplaces of the spacious rooms, and set off by pitch-loaded pine chunks. Luminously, the glow from these flames filled the rooms. Along with the singers came also parents and many children. The occasion took on the aspect of an African fete day when with African songs and folk tales they would celebrate the deeds of their heroes. To add to the spirit of festivity, I had prepared a generous variety of edibles for their pleasure, which were to be partaken of by the assembly after the singing. True, the evening turned out to be one of those rare, great joys of one's life. The singers seemed inspired, and the surge and flow of spiritual significance in their singing made me feel that I had got religion a second time. My Angel Mo' had died in 1923, but the singing of a folk song by these singers entitled "You're Tired, Chile," resurrected her and brought her presence vividly before me. As they sang, she stood there before me. The song told the story of an Aframerican woman of pre-Civil War days, who had worked hard as a slave and lived to a great age of eighty. Having been told of salvation through Christ for all those who remained faithful throughout their lives, she sat one day in the kitchen, after the dinner dishes had been cleared away, rocking in her chair and thinking on the promises of the Lord. She felt the time to be near when she would be called home to Heaven. Becoming intensely engrossed in the thought and contemplation of the event, she actually felt her moment had come. Immediately, she was surrounded by all of the heavenly hosts, who greeted her with loving enthusiasm. They saw how very weary and worn she was and with tender compassion begged her to sit down and rest awhile. But she couldn't sit down. Her restless demeanor caused the angels to inquire, *"Tell me what you waitin' for?"* To which she responded, *"I'm waitin' for my mother, I want to tell her howdy."* Well, before the singers completed this song, unashamed, I was unable to control the deep emotion upon me. I urged the singers to repeat the song many times that evening. That song is the first of the next group of ten songs which I like to call abstractions from both the Old and the New Testament, based upon the teachings of the Bible, more than on episodes from it.

1. You're Tired, Chile

(To the memory of my Angel Mo')

Arranged by Roland Hayes

Oh, sit down, sis - ter, sit down! I know you're tired,— sit down! 'Cause you come a long— way;

An' I know you're tired, sit down, chile! Sit down, an' res' a lit-'l while. Tell _____ me what you're wait-in' for. _____ I'm ___ a-wait-in' for my moth-er _____ 'Cause I want to tell her how-dy. sit down, chile! Sit down,— an' res' a lit-'l while. Oh, you

come a long way, __ An' de road is dark, __ An' I know you're tired, Sit down, chile! Sit down an' res' a lit-'l while. Oh, sit down, sis-ter, sit down! I know you're tired, sit down! 'Cause you come a long_ way, Sit down, chile! Sit down, an' res' a lit-'l

II. In-a-Dat Mornin'

Great strength moves gravely throughout the religious mysticism of this next song. Through rugged form pour the sentiments of one whose fervidly sure faith breathes an air of complete confidence and security. The Judgment holds no semblance of despair or concern for this soul. Irrespective of where the body may be buried, the soul is certain to be numbered among the redeemed "In-a-Dat Mornin'."

In-a-Dat Mornin'

Arranged by Roland Hayes

III. Plenty Good Room

Joy in anticipation of happiness, mirrored through faith, is one of the mighty pillars that support the Aframerican throughout his experiences. That portion of Scripture according to Saint John, XIV.2–3: "In my Father's house are many mansions . . . I will come again, and receive you unto myself," filled him with exuberant, rhythmic emotion. Promises forced up through love and devotion to an outburst of a song of welcome are ideally represented in the next song. Though different in the circumstances of its origin, it parallels "You're Tired, Chile" in its spontaneity, easy lilting flow and rhythmic verse.

Plenty Good Room

Arranged by Roland Hayes

plen-ty good room, plen-ty good room,_____ Good room in my Fa-ther's king-dom,

Plen-ty good room, plen-ty good room, A-jes' choose yo' seat an' set down.__

would not_ be__ a sin-na; I tell you_ de rea-son why 'Cause
would not_ be a back-slid-er;

if my_ Lord-a should call on_ me, I would-n't be read-y to die.__

65

IV. I'm Troubled

This song is closely associated with one of the rarest friendships in my life. On that day we met in Paris in 1922, Noel Sullivan had opened up for him the literature of Aframerican folk songs, and I became blessed with a friend of human and artistic value. We talked for hours about the religious folk songs of my people — their emotional, racial background, their spiritual content. Noel was so deeply moved by the significance of what he felt in these songs, which, in a sense, was his heritage as well as mine (both being American born and a part of America's traditions), that I was inspired to make for him the present musical setting. The following note on the song is taken from a book entitled *The Story of the Jubilee Singers:*

> The person who furnished this song (Mrs. Brown of Nashville, Tenn., formerly a slave) stated that she first heard it from her old father when she was a child. After he had been whipped he always went and sat upon a certain log near his cabin, and with the tears streaming down his cheeks, sang this song with so much pathos that few could listen without weeping from sympathy; and even his cruel oppressors were not wholly unmoved.[1]

[1] Marsh, J. B. T., *The Story of the Jubilee Singers.* Houghton Mifflin and Company, 1881, page 173.

I'm Troubled

(*To my great friend Noel Sullivan*)

Arranged by Roland Hayes

69

V. Heaven

The expressed joy of the next song reminds me of my ecstasy as a child which the anticipation of a brand-new pair of brass-tipped brogans at Christmas time stirred in me. That those shoes had to last me until the next Christmas made the joy of anticipation all the more keen. Heavenly shoes, long white robes and starry crowns, while taking on the hue of supernatural significance, nevertheless moved the adults of my people to like ecstatic sense. It was a thrill not to be described in mere words when they contemplated "Heaven" and the royal gifts of shoes and other adornments which are promised every true and faithful child when he reaches God's Heaven.

Heaven

Arranged by Roland Hayes

1. I got a robe, You got a robe, All-a God's chil-lun got a robe.____ When I get to heav'n goin' to
2. I got-a shoes, You got-a shoes, All-a God's chil-lun got-a shoes.____

3. I got a song, You got a song, All - a God's chil-lun got a song. _____ When _ I get to heav'n goin' to sing a new song, _ I'm goin' to sing all ___ o - ver. God's heav'n, _____ heav'n, _____ heav'n. _____ Ev -

73

VI. Steal Away

Most slaveowners considered the maintenance of illiteracy among the slaves to be for the best interest of both whites and blacks. But always an inspired leader arose here and there who learned to read the Bible, or drawing on a prodigious memory acted as a storehouse for those unable to read. Since the masters found that singing got more work out of the slaves, it became a natural outlet through which leaders could pour their Bible lore. And these historical narratives and words of wisdom were, I believe, mated to music brought from Africa, or improvised in similar mold. Such a leader amongst the slaves was my paternal great-grandfather.

The song "Steal Away" is said to be so inspired and was born in a cotton field where there were a great number of slaves hoeing cotton. The leader who always planned the date when the slaves would go secretly, after nightfall, to hear a Northern white clergyman preach the gospel of salvation through Christ would first whisper, "Steal away," to the slave next in line to him. This whispered word, spoken over rhythmic measures of hoe strokes of the choppers, was passed along the line until it reached the last individual. Work, of course, took on a more lively gait from this moment. Then the spoken word gradually took on melody which surged forth increasingly on the rhythmic verve of spirited melody of a decidedly African idiomatic pattern. The hoes were simply playing an ecstatic rhythm as an accompaniment background to the song. Now and again, the leader would halt the flow of a smoothly conceived legato to introduce a sort of recitative occasioned by the oncoming of wind or a threatened storm, which he used to stress the urgent call to the meeting. This kind of spirited melody kept up until the end of the workday. Thus the plan of the slaves to attend the religious services secretly, after nightfall, was effectively hidden from the master.

Steal Away

Arranged by Roland Hayes

VII. Po' Pilgrim

The following song is indelibly etched with the memory of the first time I heard it sung. An old wayfaring man of my race came upon our woodpile at my Angel Mo's little farm in Georgia. I was a mere child at the time. It seems that he had reached the great age when his services were of no further use to his former owners, so they turned him out. With a bundle of rags fixed to the end of a stick and a banjo under his arm, he became a wanderer.

My Angel Mo' had left me at the house to mind a younger brother. While playing in the yard I heard a voice of heartbreaking pathos. It is my first memory of having been moved by our religious folk songs. I looked, I peeped into the woodpile from behind a big cedar tree. There I saw a dejected-looking old man. He was singing, sitting on a fire log, his face resting on his right palm. The sound and sight affected me so intensely that I, not knowing why at the time, obeyed the impulse and ran into the kitchen and fetched the old man a part of the food my Mo' had left for the baby. This act was the means of gaining not only a great friend, but an early mentor.

Po' Pilgrim

mor-row, I'm striv-in' for hea-v'n my home. Some -
own me, Be - cause I am try-in' to get in.

times I'm both tossed and driv-en, Some times I know not where to

roam I've heard of a cit-y called heav'n, I've

start-ed to make it my home. My home.

molto cresc. *ff*

f

ff broadly *ritard.*

D. S.

78

VIII. Good News

Whenever the sorry lot of my people in slavery reached a near breaking point, the mind gave itself over to fevered contemplation of the promise of Christ's Kingdom. At the appointed time, God sent down a chariot of fire that took Elijah to Heaven (II Kings II.11). This fulfillment of God's promises to Elijah paralleled the promise of Christ's Kingdom as felt by the redeemed of my people. There were no doubts in their minds. Jubilation took the part when the slaves anticipated release from the tortures of existence.

It was utterly natural to identify their daily life with that of the children of Israel; to bring the Bible, Old and New Testament, into constant and immediate relationship with their experience. They would be ready with the breaking of the *"Good news, de chariot's a-comin'."* Liberty, freedom, were realities of their earth, not far removed from celestial promises found in their Bible, their religion.

Good News

Arranged by Roland Hayes

news, de cha-riot's a-com-in', Good news, de cha-riot's a-com-in', Good

news, de cha-riot's a-com in', An' I don't want it to leav'-a me be-hin'. Good

news, de cha-riot's a-com-in', Good news, de cha-riot's a-com-in', Good

news, de cha-riot's a-com-in', An' I don't want it to leav'-a me be-hin'. An' I

don' want it to leav - a me be - hin'. An' I

don' want it to leav - a me be - hin'. _____

IX. You Mus' Come in By an' Thro' de Lamb

As my people contemplated the limitless power of the Almighty He was viewed by them in terms of a fourth dimension, which is to say, no matter what one does or what powers one may muster in an effort to escape God it is not possible to do so by going over Him; irrespective of mortal man's scheming it is not possible to get under God; never mind what conniving to get around Him, that too is futile. Only one procedure is open, *"You mus' come in by an' thro' de Lamb."*

You Mus' Come in By an Thro' de Lamb

Arranged by Roland Hayes

long the heav'n-ly___ road, _____ My Sav-iour spoke un-to me,___ An'___ He
hap-pen might-y___ strange. ___ The Lord was good to Is-rael,___ An'___ His

filled my___ heart-a wid love. Oh___ He's so___ high, you can't get o-ver Him; He's
ways don't ev-er change.

too wide _____ to get a-roun' Him, You

so low___ you can't get un-der Him; He's so wide___ dat you can't get a-roun' Him, You

mus' come in___ by___ an' thro' de Lamb! _____ I ___

X. 'Roun' About de Mountain

This song is said to have originated in the Appalachian Mountain system of Tennessee. A young woman, before departing this life, acknowledged God as her Lord and Saviour. She did not die in her sins, which is the good reason for the exalted joy felt by the entire community — comprising women and children, too — as they jubilantly followed the ox-drawn cart which bore the body to its final resting place off a winding road among the hills.

'Roun' About de Mountain

(*A Recessional*)

Arranged by Roland Hayes

'Roun' a-bout de moun-tain,___ 'Roun' a-bout de moun-tain,___

My God's a-rul-in', An' she'll rise in His arms. De

Lord loves de sin-na,___ De Lord loves de sin-na___ man, De

Lord loves de sin-na, An' she'll rise in His arms.

When I— was— a sin-na,— A - seek-in'— jes' - a like you,

I went down in— de val - ley, I prayed till I come through. You

hy - po - crite, you con - cu - bine, You're placed a-mongst de swine.— You

go to God— with your lips an'— tongue, But you leave yo' heart be-hin'. De

Goin' a - roun' de moun - tain,— There I'll— take - a my stan'. I

heard de voice of Je - sus.— Thank God He's in dis - lan'. De

Lord loves de sin - na,— De Lord loves a sin - na— man,— De

Lord loves de sin - na, An' she'll rise!—

PANEL THREE
The Life of Christ

I   Prepare Me One Body

Christ's Birth, Boyhood and Ministry

II   Sister Mary Had-a But One Child

III   Lit'l Boy

IV   Live a-Humble

V   Hear de Lambs a-Cryin'?

The Passion of Our Lord

VI   The Last Supper

VII   They Led My Lord Away

VIII   He Never Said a Mumberlin' Word

IX   Did You Hear When Jesus Rose?

X   Were You There?

The Life of Christ

The salvation of man is always the great theme of masterworks in literature and art. Biblical material follows like a red thread in mankind's art works through the ages. No story appeals to man's finer creative vision as does the life of Christ. The early Christian chants, the masses of Palestrina, the passions, oratorios, masses of Bach, Handel, Beethoven — among many others — are the musical panorama of the mute majesty of the life of God on earth. With never diminishing radiance, to every succeeding generation of humanity this panorama gives life, spiritual consciousness to each in his own measure. It is small wonder that in his turn the Aframerican should find in his musical portraying of the life of Christ his most effective utterance. A social condition of the most abject humility could not help but find complete identity in a life of love, compassion and patience.

The choice of faith, the acceptance of a spiritual reality, were but the wise choice of a people who, without benefit of a philosophic tradition, recognized the all-encompassing human and divine wholeness of Truth. Jesus was their master! In that acknowledgment, that inner assurance, lay the reason for the survival of human dignity in a race that until quite recently was, as is the beast, the property of earthly masters. As it was with my own mother, so it was with the best of my race. "The master, yes, one had to acknowledge him, I belonged to him, it was the law of the land," she often told me, "but what I am, here inside me, he couldn't touch." A great, simple rule of conduct that in its earnest sincerity strikes me as nothing short of epic. It is this earnestness that lends to these songs their own nobility, their inescapable appeal. I range some of them unhesitatingly among the masterpieces of religious folk songs of all people. Humble they are, humble in origin, humble in form, humble in means. Yet, isn't the magnificent flowering fame of, for example, "Were You There?" and "He Never Said a Mumberlin' Word" rather symbolic?

That specific stamp of unforgettable dignity that gives life and reason to an individual or to a piece of music is often difficult to analyze. A sophisticated man of my acquaintance told me a luminous story of a humble charwoman in his community. Old and alone, she lives on the outskirts of town. But such is her quality that, forsaking his books, friends and rich home, he often feels impelled to visit her. He tells me, "One feels better, kinder, cleaner for having been in her presence, for having had a glimpse of her bending over her plants in her pitiful, small garden." And I am reminded of old Lewis, a janitor of my race, in a studio apartment. Nobody knew how old he was; he wouldn't or couldn't tell beyond admitting he was born in slavery. Yet I doubt if any of the many tenants will ever forget the essence of his strangely illuminating person. From the wooden partition separating the coal pile in the basement from his domicile, his spirit seemed to radiate into every room of the house, seeming to touch, as if by a miracle, human hearts. That unforgettable gift which most of us have encountered in living I believe partakes something of what we mean by salvation of man, of which my Angel Mo' speaks. To me as a human being and artist this essential and therefore timeless spirit accompanies the Aframerican Passion of Saint Matthew and Saint Mark.

As has been stated earlier in this discussion, the texts of these folk songs are a blend of versified religious paraphrases and amplifying remarks of the poets — a means of religious articulation evident in the expression of all people from time immemorial. I have had occasion already to refer to this as a quality of poetic incantation on the song sermons of my people. No less an authority than Saint Augustine is cited by Charles Burney (English critic of the eighteenth century) on that specific quality:

> When we are unable to find words worthy of the Divinity, we do well to address Him with confused sounds of joy and thanksgiving.

For to whom are such ecstatic sounds due, unless the Supreme Being? And how can we celebrate His ineffable goodness, when we are equally unable to adore Him in silence and to find any other expression of our transports, than in articulate sound?

And how true appears to me the following quotation from Milton's *Paradise Lost* in summing up the kind of ecstasy, the spring of inner singing that radiates forth from hosts of souls of my people:

> . . . All
> The multitude of Angels, with a shout
> Loud as from numbers without number, sweet
> As from bless'd voices, uttering joy, heav'n rung
> With jubilee, and loud Hosannas fill'd
> Th' eternal regions.

It is curious how in our times such religious poetic creations as the Hebrew chant, Palestrina, Lassus, Gregorian chant, the great masses of Bach, Beethoven, the monumental Biblical oratorios, the religious folk songs of my people, have become concert fare, and sometimes museum pieces, that we study with the rational abstract aloofness of the scholar and student. Yet it would seem to me that only in finding our way back to the simple truth to which these human documents testify can we find the key to the spirit inherent in them. By lending our ear to the continuity, perseverance and simple feeling in them, we may find, as the artist in his quest for perfection, the heartstring of their meaning, with which lives the meaning of the words of Christ.

I. Prepare Me One Body

A sort of prologue to "The Life of Christ" series is the beautiful Aframerican folk song, "Prepare Me One Body." The original of the text of this song is not to be found in any of the Gospels and Prophecies. But I believe it to be a dramatization by our early Aframerican preachers of such Biblical elements as are found in Saint Paul's Epistle to the Philippians (II.5–8):

> . . . Christ Jesus: who . . . took upon him the form of a servant . . . was made in the likeness of men . . . humbled himself . . . became obedient unto death, even the death of the cross.

Prepare Me One Body

Arranged by Roland Hayes

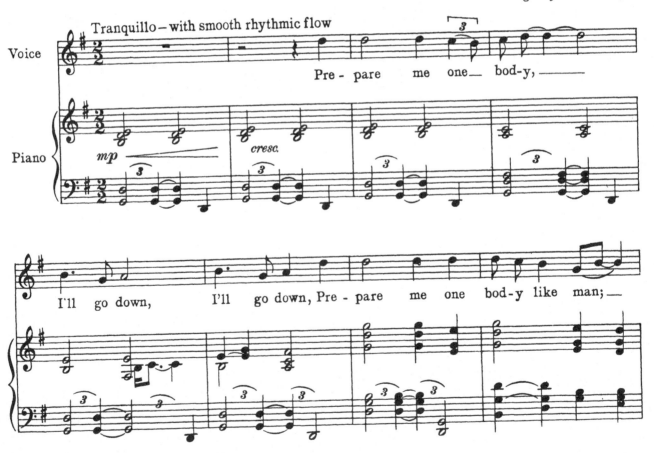

I'll go down an' die. The man of sor-rows, sin-ner, see;__ I'll go down, I'll go down, He__ died for you an'__ He died for me;__ I'll go down an' die. Pre - pare me, Lord, one__ bod-y!__ Pre-pare me one bod-y, like man!__ I'll go down an' die!

97

II. Sister Mary Had-a But One Child

From the earliest memories of my boyhood, this song has remained with me as one of few Aframerican folk songs dealing with the Nativity. I believe it is of very early Aframerican origin in the United States, and bears the stamp rhythmically and melodically of African musical idiom. On listening to its *berceuse*-like rhythm, one should not find it hard to imagine an old crude manger in a Bethlehem stable. But to me, the rocking was not that of Mother Mary's hand, but of some mysteriously roving, supernatural wind which swayed the ancient walls to which the Holy Child's crib was pegged.

Sister Mary Had-a But One Child

(*Nativity*)

Arranged by Roland Hayes

rocked Him in the wea-ry land.

1. O
2. An(*to* §)

(*Verse 2 at* §)

Three wise men - a to Je - ru - sa-lem came,_ They'd trav - elled_ ver - y far._

più f

They said, "Where is_ He_ born_ King of the Jews,_ For

we have - a - seen His star?"_ King He - rod's_ heart was

trou - bled, —— He mar-velled but his face was grim. He said,

"Tell me— where the Child may be found, I'll— go and— wor - ship

Him, — I'll go and— wor - ship Him." *D. S.* Sis - ter

an - gel— ap-peared to— Jo - seph,— And gave him- a this-a com-mand.—

più f

"A - rise ye, take - a your wife and child, Go flee in - to E - gypt land. For yon - der comes old He - rod, A wick - ed man and bold. He's slay - in' all the chil - lun From six to eight - a days old, From six to eight - a days old."

Sis-ter Ma-ry— had-a but one child,—

Born in Beth-le-hem.— And-a ev-er-y time-a the-a

ba-by cried, She'd-a rocked Him in the wea-ry land,— She'd-a

rocked Him in the wea-ry land.—

ppp

III. Lit'l Boy

Of early origin and decidedly African is "Lit'l Boy, How Ole Are You?" a solo-type folk song. This particular song was sung to me by my old friend, William L. Shelton. He had once heard it sung by a traveling Aframerican evangelist. Because of the native African quality, rhythmically and idiomatically, I have written its accompaniment in a pure African design suggested by an idiomatic rhythmic pattern given me by Nigeria West Africans in London. I have arranged it to retain as nearly as possible its original flavor, through our conventional harmonic form, and conventional instrument, the piano.

Lit'l Boy

(Christ in the Temple)

Exclamatory—Voice ad lib.

Arranged by Roland Hayes

Law-yers and doc-tors were a - mazed, and had to give the Lit-'l Boy the praise.

"Lit-'l Boy, how ole are you? Lit-'l Boy, how ole are you?

Lit-'l Boy,— how ole are you?" "Sir, I'm on-ly twelve years old."

Law-yers and doc-tors stood and won-dered, As though they had been struck by thun-der. Then

they de - cid - ed while they won-dered, That all man-kind must come un-der.

"Lit-'l Boy, how ole are you? Lit-'l Boy, how ole are you?

Lit-'l Boy,_ how ole are you?" "Sir, I'm on - ly twelve years old!" The

last time_ the Lit-'l Boy was seen, He_ was stand-in' on_ Mount O - li - vet green.

When He'd dis-per-sed of the crowd,— He en-tered up in-to a cloud.—

"Lit-'l Boy,— how ole are you? Lit-'l Boy,— how ole are you?

Lit-'l Boy,— how ole are you?" "Sir, I'm on - ly twelve years old?"

IV. Live a-Humble

Jesus, the true example of humility, inspires men to develop strength for forbearance. The Aframerican slave learned and practiced it continually. It is one of the saving graces of his nature, that enabled him to emerge from his trials with resilience and flexibility. The song "Live a-Humble" tells of watching daily the temptations of this life; of continuing faithfully active in the sense of our duties to God and one another; of working, that we may be ready to receive Him when He comes. Also, it treats of Jesus's healing of the sick; restoring sight to the blind; enabling the crippled to walk.

Live a-Humble

(*He Healed the Sick*)

Arranged by Roland Hayes

A-live a - hum-ble,— hum-ble,————

Hum-ble—your-self, de bell's-a done-a rung. A-live a - hum-ble,— hum-ble,————

Hum-ble—your-self, de bell's done rung. Glo - ry an' hon-or!——— (Praise King Je- sus!) Glo-

- ry an' hon-or;— Praise de Lamb. Oh,— my Lord's done jes' what He said,— my Lord, He

meno mosso e sempre col canto

healed de sick an'_ He raised de dead. A-live a - hum-ble,___ hum-ble, ___

a tempo

Hum-ble_ your-self, de bell's done rung. Did you ev - er_ see_ such a

meno mosso

man as_ God, Who gave up His Son_ for to come an'_ die! He gave up His Son_ for to

crescendo **f** *espressivo grande* — — — — *a tempo*

come an'_ die, Jes' to save my soul from a burn-ing_ fire. A-live a - hum-ble,___

crescendo col canto *a tempo*

hum-ble,— Hum-ble— your-self, de bell's done rung.— Glo - ry an' hon-or!—

— Glo - ry an' hon-or,— Praise de Lamb. A- live a - hum-ble,—

(Praise King Je-sus!)

hum-ble,— Hum-ble your-self, de bell's done rung. A- live a - hum-ble,—

hum-ble,——————— Hum-ble— your-self, de bell's done rung.——

ritardando

V. Hear de Lambs a-Cryin'?

Jesus sensed, always knew, the frailty of humankind and sought with utmost compassion to help man in his weaknesses. Thus He questions Peter, His disciple, with respect to his faithfulness and exhorts him to do his full duty as befitting a true disciple. So gently, so beseechingly He inquires: *"Peter, if you love me, feed-a my sheep!"*

The melody has a Hebraic flavor that moves in a tender minor mode.

Hear de Lambs a-Cryin'?

Arranged by Roland Hayes

The Passion of Our Lord

"The first appearance of dramatic dialogue in the services of the Church," according to Paul Henry Láng, "may be traced back to the ninth century. . . . The dramatic atmosphere was not restricted to the dialogue. . . . The incidents which mark the birth of Christ, the adoration of the shepherds, and of the Magi, the wrath of Herod, and the massacre of the Innocents, provided the material for the Christmas cycle; the Resurrection that for the other important cycle of Easter. From the simple dialogue sung at Eastertime developed the colossal literature of the Passion." [1]

The traditional form presented by the Church is the mass — Kyrie, Gloria, Credo, Sanctus, Benedictus, and Agnus Dei, all of which were retained by Luther. The act of sacrifice (the Offertorium), being typically Catholic, had been supplanted by the sermon. Were the song sermons of my people perhaps an adapted continuation of the German sermon of Reformation days, or rather a kind of Pachelion, a form of sermon in music?

Making the supreme sacrifice of human life to a noble purpose, in some of the African kingdoms, I am told, is a common occurrence. It is said that Africans in these kingdoms of Central Africa vie with each other for the honor; that individuals chosen to make the sacrifice experience exaltation increas-

[1] *Music in Western Civilization.* W. W. Norton & Company, Inc., New York, 1941.

112

ingly during the interim of awaiting the sacrificial hour. Thus it becomes quite understandable that religious leaders amongst Africans found little or no difficulty in winning them to immediate, favorable reaction when they related the story of the supreme sacrifice which Jesus Christ made for the salvation of all humanity. The news of Jesus's loving and serving those who hated and abused Him was no unusual news to the Aframerican slave. The story of Jesus in Gethsemane and His experience on the Cross did grip the imagination of my people and stirred them to emotional heights such as are shown in their songs of exaltation under the tragic experiences of excruciating pain and intense suffering at the hands of some of their cruel masters.

The high principle revealed through the example which Jesus made of Himself by washing His disciples' feet at a moment when He was fully aware that one of the twelve disciples would presently betray Him moved by people mightily. "You call me master and Lord. . . . If I then, your Lord and Master, have washed your feet; ye also ought to wash one another's feet. For I have given you an example, that ye should do as I have done to you" (Saint John XIII.13–15).

That my people grasped the meaning of Christ's teachings is not only mirrored through their lives and example as human loving beings; it is particularly reflected in their songs. You may search the entire collection of Aframerican religious folk songs extant — which number in the hundreds — and you will not find one word of hate or malice anywhere expressed in them. The Aframerican has pictured with understanding the spiritual essence, the tender, but poignant, "Passion of Our Lord" in poetry and music.

The five songs in the "Passion" group of songs are not used consecutively in the Aframericans' church service as they appear here, but it may be of interest to realize how effective these songs can be on an Easter observance occasion.

VI. The Last Supper

The opening words of the first part of this song — which lead into the refrain, "*My time is come*" — bring us to the point of "The Last Supper" where Jesus indicates His betrayal by one of the twelve disciples. Then, immediately following the refrain, "*My time is come*," we perceive the Aframerican's extraordinary grasp of human values, as well as spiritual essences, as is highlighted by his depiction (in words and music) of the mood where Jesus is at prayer in the Garden of Gethsemane.

The utter dejection of mortal man in the moment of such distress was never more movingly pictured in words and musical cadence than in what the originator of this song has given. There is the silent throb of a troubled heart felt as inner pulse, actually an undertone (in measured tempo) of the tragic mood sounding through the words of Jesus — "*Simon! Sleepest thou?*" — when He returned from prayer and found His disciples all asleep.

Imagine an entire congregation sitting in rapt attention under the hypnotic spell of an eloquent Aframerican preacher (feet a-patting out a supersoft rhythm) in company with spiritually electrified bodies that sway (clockwise) forward and backwards, keeping the mood created by the preacher alive, and heightening, as he with masterful imagery vividly picturizes the story of the whole of the tragic garden scene.

In the music setting under the melody and words in the Garden of Gethsemane, I have fixed, sustained minor chords tied together that hold throughout several measures. The rhythmic pulse embracing four counts to the measure is represented in quarter notes in the bass clef and below it.

The Last Supper

Arranged by Roland Hayes

-sus was a-sit-tin' at the last Pass-o-ver. John, he rest-ed_ up-on _ His shoul-der._ Je-sus said one_ word_ that seemed to blight. He said, "One of_ you_ goin' to be-tray me to-night."_

Mark cried out, "Lord, is it ___ I?" ___ James cried out, ___ "Lord is ___ it ___ I?" ___

Then Je-sus ___ said, "A-look an' ___ see ___ him ___ dat dip in ___ de dish-a wid ___ me."

Andante

My time is come, my time is come, Oh, my time is come!

Then Jesus with his disciples Simon-Peter, and others went into the garden. Jesus said to them, "Tarry ye here, while I go and pray." Then when Jesus on returning found his disciples asleep He said:

116

quasi recitativo – ad lib.

Si - mon! ____ Si ____ mon!

Sleep - est thou? Si ____ mon! Could'st

Thou not watch one hour? Si - mon! The

spi - rit ___ is will - ing, ___ but ___ the flesh is weak. _____

My time is come, my time is come, Oh,— my time is come,— I'm boun' to pay de debt I owe.

l.h.

VII. They Led My Lord Away

When Jesus had come the third time to His disciples, He said, "It is enough, the hour is come; behold, the Son of man is betrayed into the hands of sinners."

"While he yet spake" (Saint Mark XIV.41) Judas and his gang appeared.

It was the kiss of Judas on approaching Jesus that was the cue for the high priest and his men to seize Him.

They Led My Lord Away

Andante con moto

with great pathos

Arranged by Roland Hayes

Voice

They — led my Lord a - way, a - way, a -

Piano

way, — They led my Lord a - way. Oh tell me where to

find Him.

They led Him up to
Pi - late said, "I

VIII. He Never Said a Mumberlin' Word [1]

But Christ's mission had to be fulfilled. They crucified Him.

[1] In respect both to its music and to its marvelous words, this song is a master work among all Aframerican religious folk songs. It definitely was the creation of an African who came to these shores already an accomplished bard. This particular version is a song sermon, emphatically a solo. He whom this poet-musician so poignantly reveres in this song is the only being he would call master.

He Never Said a Mumberlin' Word

Andante molto

Arranged by Roland Hayes

Voice

Piano

Was-n't it _ a pi-ty an' a shame!_ An' He nev-er said a

mum-ber-lin' word. _ Was-n't it _ a pi-ty an' a shame!_

_ An' He nev-er said a mum-ber-lin' word, _ Oh_ not a word,

_ not a word, _ not a word! _ Dey nailed Him to_

_ de tree! _ An' He nev-er said a mum-ber-lin' word! _ Dey

nailed Him to_____ de tree!____ An' He nev-er said a

IX. Did You Hear When Jesus Rose?

"In the end of the Sabbath, as it began to dawn toward the first day of the week, came Mary Magdalene and the other Mary to see the sepulchre. . . . And the angel answered and said unto the women . . . He is not here; for he is risen, as he said . . . go quickly, and tell his disciples. . . . And she [Mary Magdalene] went and told them . . . afterwards he [Christ] appeared unto the eleven. . . . So then after the Lord had spoken unto them, he was received up into heaven, and sat on the right hand of God."

The minor mode in which this song is cast does not set free, entirely, the ecstatic joy expressed at the resurrection of our Lord. I can well imagine that the originator of the song had in mind that to do so would have had an overshadowing effect of the more poignant meaning — the triumph of Jesus over death — which this semi-minor musical mode preserves.

Did You Hear When Jesus Rose?

Arranged by Roland Hayes

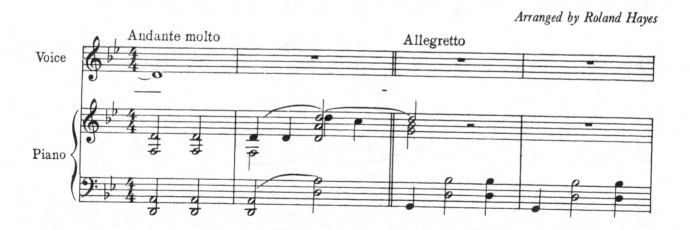

soul from Hell, _____ An' de Son freed me from sin.

Chil-lun, did you hear when Je - sus rose, did you hear_ when Je - sus

rose? _____ Did you hear when Je - sus rose? _____ He

rose an' as-cend-ed on high. _____

rall.

X. Were You There?

The Aframerican poets and musicians set Christ's death on the Cross apart from that of all others in that only through His death did all mankind fall heir to salvation and life eternal.

But, often, man in the midst of his tranquillity and enjoyment of promised redemption through Christ forgets that he, an heir to life eternal, has definite duties to perform thereto before he can claim the promised reward.

Are we then, as human beings, keeping ourselves in a constant state of awareness in the sense of, for instance, a daily exercise and practice of "being our brothers' keeper"? Here, as the next song of this collection envisions, we of all races and of every creed are brought together in one embrace of the *all-important* question; not so much, however, *"Were you there when they crucified my Lord?"* but — in the sense of the responsibilities which this death places upon us to love and serve God and one another — *Are you there?*

"SOMETIMES IT CAUSES ME TO TREMBLE!"

Were You There?

Arranged by Roland Hayes

some-times it caus-es me to trem-ble,

trem - ble, trem - ble! Were you there when they

cru - ci - fied my Lord?_____ Were you

Dover Piano and Keyboard Editions

Albeniz, Isaac, IBERIA AND ESPAÑA: Two Complete Works for Solo Piano. Spanish composer's greatest piano works in authoritative editions. Includes the popular "Tango." 192pp. 9 x 12. 0-486-25367-8

Bach, Johann Sebastian, COMPLETE KEYBOARD TRANSCRIPTIONS OF CONCERTOS BY BAROQUE COMPOSERS. Sixteen concertos by Vivaldi, Telemann and others, transcribed for solo keyboard instruments. Bach-Gesellschaft edition. 128pp. 9⅜ x 12¼. 0-486-25529-8

Bach, Johann Sebastian, COMPLETE PRELUDES AND FUGUES FOR ORGAN. All 25 of Bach's complete sets of preludes and fugues (i.e. compositions written as pairs), from the authoritative Bach-Gesellschaft edition. 168pp. 8⅜ x 11. 0-486-24816-X

Bach, Johann Sebastian, ITALIAN CONCERTO, CHROMATIC FANTASIA AND FUGUE AND OTHER WORKS FOR KEYBOARD. Sixteen of Bach's best-known, most-performed and most-recorded works for the keyboard, reproduced from the authoritative Bach-Gesellschaft edition. 112pp. 9 x 12. 0-486-25387-2

Bach, Johann Sebastian, KEYBOARD MUSIC. Bach-Gesellschaft edition. For harpsichord, piano, other keyboard instruments. English Suites, French Suites, Six Partitas, Goldberg Variations, Two-Part Inventions, Three-Part Sinfonias. 312pp. 8⅛ x 11. 0-486-22360-4

Bach, Johann Sebastian, ORGAN MUSIC. Bach-Gesellschaft edition. 93 works. 6 Trio Sonatas, German Organ Mass, Orgelbüchlein, Six Schubler Chorales, 18 Choral Preludes. 357pp. 8⅛ x 11. 0-486-22359-0

Bach, Johann Sebastian, TOCCATAS, FANTASIAS, PASSACAGLIA AND OTHER WORKS FOR ORGAN. Over 20 best-loved works including Toccata and Fugue in D Minor, BWV 565; Passacaglia and Fugue in C Minor, BWV 582, many more. Bach-Gesellschaft edition. 176pp. 9 x 12. 0-486-25403-8

Bach, Johann Sebastian, TWO- AND THREE-PART INVENTIONS. Reproduction of original autograph ms. Edited by Eric Simon. 62pp. 8⅛ x 11. 0-486-21982-8

Bach, Johann Sebastian, THE WELL-TEMPERED CLAVIER: Books I and II, Complete. All 48 preludes and fugues in all major and minor keys. Authoritative Bach-Gesellschaft edition. Explanation of ornaments in English, tempo indications, music corrections. 208pp. 9⅜ x 12¼. 0-486-24532-2

Bartók, Béla, PIANO MUSIC OF BÉLA BARTÓK, Series I. New, definitive Archive Edition incorporating composer's corrections. Includes *Funeral March* from *Kossuth, Fourteen Bagatelles,* Bartók's break to modernism. 167pp. 9 x 12. (Available in U.S. only) 0-486-24108-4

Bartók, Béla, PIANO MUSIC OF BÉLA BARTÓK, Series II. Second in the Archive Edition incorporating composer's corrections. 85 short pieces *For Children, Two Elegies, Two Romanian Dances,* etc. 192pp. 9 x 12. (Available in U.S. only) 0-486-24109-2

Beethoven, Ludwig van, BAGATELLES, RONDOS AND OTHER SHORTER WORKS FOR PIANO. Most popular and most performed shorter works, including Rondo a capriccio in G and Andante in F. Breitkopf & Härtel edition. 128pp. 9⅜ x 12¼. 0-486-25392-9

Beethoven, Ludwig van, COMPLETE PIANO SONATAS. All sonatas in fine Schenker edition, with fingering, analytical material. One of best modern editions. 615pp. 9 x 12. Two-vol. set. 0-486-23134-8, 0-486-23135-6

Beethoven, Ludwig van, COMPLETE VARIATIONS FOR SOLO PIANO, Ludwig van Beethoven. Contains all 21 sets of Beethoven's piano variations, including the extremely popular *Diabelli Variations, Op. 120.* 240pp. 9⅜ x 12¼. 0-486-25188-8

Beethoven, Ludwig van, BEETHOVEN MASTERPIECES FOR SOLO PIANO: 25 Works. Twenty-five popular pieces include the Sonata in C-sharp Minor, Op. 27, No. 2 ("Moonlight"); Sonata in D Minor, Op. 31, No. 2 ("Tempest"); 32 Variations in C Minor; Andante in F Major; Rondo Capriccio, Op. 129; Fantasia, Op. 77; and popular bagatelles, rondos, minuets, and other works. 160pp. 9 x 12. 0-486-43570-9

Blesh, Rudi (ed.), CLASSIC PIANO RAGS. Best ragtime music (1897–1922) by Scott Joplin, James Scott, Joseph F. Lamb, Tom Turpin, nine others. 364pp. 9 x 12. Introduction by Blesh. 0-486-20469-3

Brahms, Johannes, COMPLETE SHORTER WORKS FOR SOLO PIANO. All solo music not in other two volumes. Waltzes, Scherzo in E Flat Minor, Eight Pieces, Rhapsodies, Fantasies, Intermezzi, etc. Vienna Gesellschaft der Musikfreunde. 180pp. 9 x 12. 0-486-22651-4

Brahms, Johannes, COMPLETE SONATAS AND VARIATIONS FOR SOLO PIANO. All sonatas, five variations on themes from Schumann, Paganini, Handel, etc. Vienna Gesellschaft der Musikfreunde edition. 178pp. 9 x 12. 0-486-22650-6

Brahms, Johannes, COMPLETE TRANSCRIPTIONS, CADENZAS AND EXERCISES FOR SOLO PIANO. Vienna Gesellschaft der Musikfreunde edition, vol. 15. Studies after Chopin, Weber, Bach; gigues, sarabandes; 10 Hungarian dances, etc. 178pp. 9 x 12. 0-486-22652-2

Byrd, William, MY LADY NEVELLS BOOKE OF VIRGINAL MUSIC. 42 compositions in modern notation from 1591 ms. For any keyboard instrument. 245pp. 8⅛ x 11. 0-486-22246-2

Chopin, Frédéric, COMPLETE BALLADES, IMPROMPTUS AND SONATAS. The four Ballades, four Impromptus and three Sonatas. Authoritative Mikuli edition. 192pp. 9 x 12. 0-486-24164-5

Chopin, Frédéric, COMPLETE MAZURKAS, Frédéric Chopin. 51 best-loved compositions, reproduced directly from the authoritative Kistner edition edited by Carl Mikuli. 160pp. 9 x 12. 0-486-25548-4

Chopin, Frédéric, COMPLETE PRELUDES AND ETUDES FOR SOLO PIANO. All 25 Preludes and all 27 Etudes by greatest piano music composer. Authoritative Mikuli edition. 192pp. 9 x 12. 0-486-24052-5

Chopin, Frédéric, FANTASY IN F MINOR, BARCAROLLE, BERCEUSE AND OTHER WORKS FOR SOLO PIANO. 15 works, including one of the greatest of the Romantic period, the Fantasy in F Minor, Op. 49, reprinted from the authoritative German edition prepared by Chopin's student, Carl Mikuli. 224pp. 8⅜ x 11¼. 0-486-25950-1

Chopin, Frédéric, CHOPIN MASTERPIECES FOR SOLO PIANO: 46 Works. Includes Ballade No. 1 in G Minor, Berceuse, 3 ecossaises, 5 etudes, Fantaisie-Impromptu, Marche Funèbre, 8 mazurkas, 7 nocturnes, 3 polonaises, 9 preludes, Scherzo No. 2 in B-flat Minor, and 6 waltzes. Authoritative sources. 224pp. 9 x 12. 0-486-40150-2

Chopin, Frédéric, NOCTURNES AND POLONAISES. 20 *Nocturnes* and 11 *Polonaises* reproduced from the authoritative Mikuli edition for pianists, students, and musicologists. Commentary. 224pp. 9 x 12. 0-486-24564-0

Chopin, Frédéric, WALTZES AND SCHERZOS. All of the Scherzos and nearly all (20) of the Waltzes from the authoritative Mikuli edition. Editorial commentary. 160pp. 9 x 12. 0-486-24316-8

Cofone, Charles J. F. (ed.), ELIZABETH ROGERS HIR VIRGINALL BOOKE. All 112 pieces from noted 1656 manuscript, most never before published. Composers include Thomas Brewer, William Byrd, Orlando Gibbons, etc. Calligraphy by editor. 125pp. 9 x 12. 0-486-23138-0

Dover Piano and Keyboard Editions

Couperin, François, KEYBOARD WORKS/Series One: Ordres I–XIII; Series Two: Ordres XIV–XXVII and Miscellaneous Pieces. Over 200 pieces. Reproduced directly from edition prepared by Johannes Brahms and Friedrich Chrysander. Total of 496pp. 8⅛ x 11.
Series I: 0-486-25795-9; Series II: 0-486-25796-7

Debussy, Claude, COMPLETE PRELUDES, Books 1 and 2. 24 evocative works that reveal the essence of Debussy's genius for musical imagery, among them many of the composer's most famous piano compositions. Glossary of French terms. 128pp. 8⅜ x 11¼. 0-486-25970-6

Debussy, Claude, DEBUSSY MASTERPIECES FOR SOLO PIANO: 20 Works. From France's most innovative and influential composer–a rich compilation of works that include "Golliwogg's cakewalk," "Engulfed cathedral," "Clair de lune," and 17 others. 128pp. 9 x 12. 0-486-42425-1

Debussy, Claude, PIANO MUSIC 1888–1905. Deux Arabesques, Suite Bergamesque, Masques, first series of Images, etc. Nine others, in corrected editions. 175pp. 9⅜ x 12¼. 0-486-22771-5

Dvořák, Antonín, HUMORESQUES AND OTHER WORKS FOR SOLO PIANO. Humoresques, Op. 101, complete, Silhouettes, Op. 8, Poetic Tone Pictures, Theme with Variations, Op. 36, 4 Slavonic Dances, more. 160pp. 9 x 12. 0-486-28355-0

de Falla, Manuel, AMOR BRUJO AND EL SOMBRERO DE TRES PICOS FOR SOLO PIANO. With these two popular ballets, *El Amor Brujo* (Love, the Magician) and *El Sombrero de Tres Picos* (The Three-Cornered Hat), Falla brought the world's attention to the music of Spain. The composer himself made these arrangements of the complete ballets for piano solo. xii+132pp. 9 x 12. 0-486-44170-9

Fauré, Gabriel, COMPLETE PRELUDES, IMPROMPTUS AND VALSES-CAPRICES. Eighteen elegantly wrought piano works in authoritative editions. Only one-volume collection available. 144pp. 9 x 12. (Not available in France or Germany) 0-486-25789-4

Fauré, Gabriel, NOCTURNES AND BARCAROLLES FOR SOLO PIANO. 12 nocturnes and 12 barcarolles reprinted from authoritative French editions. 208pp. 9⅜ x 12¼. (Not available in France or Germany) 0-486-27955-3

Feofanov, Dmitry (ed.), RARE MASTERPIECES OF RUSSIAN PIANO MUSIC: Eleven Pieces by Glinka, Balakirev, Glazunov and Others. Glinka's *Prayer,* Balakirev's *Reverie,* Liapunov's *Transcendental Etude, Op. 11, No. 10,* and eight others–full, authoritative scores from Russian texts. 144pp. 9 x 12. 0-486-24659-0

Franck, César, ORGAN WORKS. Composer's best-known works for organ, including Six Pieces, Trois Pieces, and Trois Chorals. Oblong format for easy use at keyboard. Authoritative Durand edition. 208pp. 11⅜ x 8¼. 0-486-25517-4

Gottschalk, Louis M., PIANO MUSIC. 26 pieces (including covers) by early 19th-century American genius. "Bamboula," "The Banjo," other Creole, Negro-based material, through elegant salon music. 301pp. 9¼ x 12. 0-486-21683-7

Granados, Enrique, GOYESCAS, SPANISH DANCES AND OTHER WORKS FOR SOLO PIANO. Great Spanish composer's most admired, most performed suites for the piano, in definitive Spanish editions. 176pp. 9 x 12. 0-486-25481-X

Grieg, Edvard, COMPLETE LYRIC PIECES FOR PIANO. All 66 pieces from Grieg's ten sets of little mood pictures for piano, favorites of generations of pianists. 224pp. 9⅜ x 12¼. 0-486-26176-X

Handel, G. F., KEYBOARD WORKS FOR SOLO INSTRUMENTS. 35 neglected works from Handel's vast oeuvre, originally jotted down as improvisations. Includes Eight Great Suites, others. New sequence. 174pp. 9⅜ x 12¼. 0-486-24338-9

Haydn, Joseph, COMPLETE PIANO SONATAS. 52 sonatas reprinted from authoritative Breitkopf & Härtel edition. Extremely clear and readable; ample space for notes, analysis. 464pp. 9⅜ x 12¼.
Vol. I: 0-486-24726-0; Vol. II: 0-486-24727-9

Jasen, David A. (ed.), RAGTIME GEMS: Original Sheet Music for 25 Ragtime Classics. Includes original sheet music and covers for 25 rags, including three of Scott Joplin's finest: "Searchlight Rag," "Rose Leaf Rag," and "Fig Leaf Rag." 122pp. 9 x 12. 0-486-25248-5

Joplin, Scott, COMPLETE PIANO RAGS. All 38 piano rags by the acknowledged master of the form, reprinted from the publisher's original editions complete with sheet music covers. Introduction by David A. Jasen. 208pp. 9 x 12. 0-486-25807-6

Liszt, Franz, ANNÉES DE PÈLERINAGE, COMPLETE. Authoritative Russian edition of piano masterpieces: *Première Année (Suisse): Deuxième Année (Italie)* and *Venezia e Napoli; Troisième Année,* other related pieces. 288pp. 9⅜ x 12¼. 0-486-25627-8

Liszt, Franz, BEETHOVEN SYMPHONIES NOS. 6–9 TRANSCRIBED FOR SOLO PIANO. Includes Symphony No. 6 in F major, Op. 68, "Pastorale"; Symphony No. 7 in A major, Op. 92; Symphony No. 8 in F major, Op. 93; and Symphony No. 9 in D minor, Op. 125, "Choral." A memorable tribute from one musical genius to another. 224pp. 9 x 12. 0-486-41884-7

Liszt, Franz, COMPLETE ETUDES FOR SOLO PIANO, Series I: Including the Transcendental Etudes, edited by Busoni. Also includes Etude in 12 Exercises, 12 Grandes Etudes and Mazeppa. Breitkopf & Härtel edition. 272pp. 8⅜ x 11¼. 0-486-25815-7

Liszt, Franz, COMPLETE ETUDES FOR SOLO PIANO, Series II: Including the Paganini Etudes and Concert Etudes, edited by Busoni. Also includes Morceau de Salon, Ab Irato. Breitkopf & Härtel edition. 192pp. 8⅜ x 11¼. 0-486-25816-5

Liszt, Franz, COMPLETE HUNGARIAN RHAPSODIES FOR SOLO PIANO. All 19 Rhapsodies reproduced directly from authoritative Russian edition. All headings, footnotes translated to English. 224pp. 8⅜ x 11¼. 0-486-24744-9

Liszt, Franz, LISZT MASTERPIECES FOR SOLO PIANO: 13 Works. Masterworks by the supreme piano virtuoso of the 19th century: *Hungarian Rhapsody No. 2 in C-sharp minor, Consolation No. 3 in D-Flat major, Liebestraum No. 3 in A-flat major, La Campanella* (Paganini Etude No. 3), and nine others. 128pp. 9 x 12. 0-486-41379-9

Liszt, Franz, MEPHISTO WALTZ AND OTHER WORKS FOR SOLO PIANO. Rapsodie Espagnole, Liebestraüme Nos. 1–3, Valse Oubliée No. 1, Nuages Gris, Polonaises Nos. 1 and 2, Grand Galop Chromatique, more. 192pp. 8⅜ x 11¼. 0-486-28147-7

Liszt, Franz, PIANO TRANSCRIPTIONS FROM FRENCH AND ITALIAN OPERAS. Virtuoso transformations of themes by Mozart, Verdi, Bellini, other masters, into unforgettable music for piano. Published in association with American Liszt Society. 247pp. 9 x 12. 0-486-24273-0

Maitland, J. Fuller, Squire, W. B. (eds.), THE FITZWILLIAM VIRGINAL BOOK. Famous early 17th-century collection of keyboard music, 300 works by Morley, Byrd, Bull, Gibbons, etc. Modern notation. Total of 938pp. 8⅜ x 11. Two-vol. set. 0-486-21068-5, 0-486-21069-3

Medtner, Nikolai, COMPLETE FAIRY TALES FOR SOLO PIANO. Thirty-eight complex, surprising pieces by an underrated Russian 20th-century Romantic whose music is more cerebral and harmonically adventurous than Rachmaninoff's. 272pp. 9 x 12. (Available in U.S. only) 0-486-41683-6

*Available from your music dealer or write for **free** Music Catalog to*
Dover Publications, Inc., Dept. MUBI, 31 East 2nd Street, Mineola, NY 11501
*Visit us online at **www.doverpublications.com***

Dover Popular Songbooks

(Arranged by title)

ALEXANDER'S RAGTIME BAND AND OTHER FAVORITE SONG HITS, 1901–1911, David A. Jasen (ed.). Fifty vintage popular songs America still sings, reprinted in their entirety from the original editions. Introduction. 224pp. 9 x 12. (Available in U.S. only) 0-486-25331-7

AMERICAN BALLADS AND FOLK SONGS, John A. Lomax and Alan Lomax. Over 200 songs, music and lyrics: "Frankie and Albert," "John Henry," "Frog Went a-Courtin'," "Down in the Valley," "Skip to My Lou," other favorites. Notes on each song. 672pp. 5⅜ x 8½. 0-486-28276-7

AMERICAN FOLK SONGS FOR GUITAR, David Nadal (ed.). Forty-nine classics for beginning and intermediate guitar players, including "Beautiful Dreamer," "Amazing Grace," "Aura Lee," "John Henry," "The Gift to Be Simple," "Go Down, Moses," "Sweet Betsy from Pike," "Short'nin Bread," many more. 96pp. 9 x 12. 0-486-41700-X

THE AMERICAN SONG TREASURY: 100 Favorites, Theodore Raph (ed.). Complete piano arrangements, guitar chords, and lyrics for 100 best-loved tunes, "Buffalo Gals," "Oh, Suzanna," "Clementine," "Camptown Races," and much more. 416pp. 8¼ x 11. 0-486-25222-1

"BEALE STREET" AND OTHER CLASSIC BLUES: 38 Works, 1901–1921, David A. Jasen (ed.). "St. Louis Blues," "The Hesitating Blues," "Down Home Blues," "Jelly Roll Blues," "Railroad Blues," and many more. Reproduced directly from rare sheet music (including original covers). Introduction. 160pp. 9 x 12. (Available in U.S. only) 0-486-40183-9

THE CIVIL WAR SONGBOOK, Richard Crawford (ed.). 37 songs: "Battle Hymn of the Republic," "Drummer Boy of Shiloh," "Dixie," and 34 more. 157pp. 9 x 12. 0-486-23422-3

CIVIL WAR SONGS AND BALLADS FOR GUITAR, Compiled, Edited, and Arranged by Jerry Silverman. 41 favorites, among them "Marching Through Georgia," "The Battle Hymn of the Republic," "Tenting on the Old Camp Ground," and "When Johnny Comes Marching Home." 160pp. 9 x 12. 0-486-41902-9

FAVORITE CHRISTMAS CAROLS, selected and arranged by Charles J. F. Cofone. Title, music, first verse and refrain of 34 traditional carols in handsome calligraphy; also subsequent verses and other information in type. 79pp. 8⅜ x 11. 0-486-20445-6

FAVORITE SONGS OF THE NINETIES, Robert Fremont (ed.). 88 favorites: "Ta-Ra-Ra-Boom-De-Aye," "The Band Played on," "Bird in a Gilded Cage," etc. 401pp. 9 x 12. 0-486-21536-9

500 BEST-LOVED SONG LYRICS, Ronald Herder (ed.). Complete lyrics for well-known folk songs, hymns, popular and show tunes, more. "Oh Susanna," "The Battle Hymn of the Republic," "When Johnny Comes Marching Home," hundreds more. Indispensable for singalongs, parties, family get-togethers, etc. 416pp. 5⅜ x 8½. 0-486-29725-X

MY FIRST BOOK OF AMERICAN FOLK SONGS: 20 Favorite Pieces in Easy Piano Arrangements, Bergerac (ed.). Expert settings of traditional favorites by a well-known composer and arranger for young pianists: *Amazing Grace, Blue Tail Fly, Sweet Betsy from Pike*, many more. 48pp. 8¼ x 11. 0-486-28885-4

MY FIRST BOOK OF CHRISTMAS SONGS: 20 Favorite Songs in Easy Piano Arrangements, Bergerac (ed.). Beginners will love playing these beloved favorites in easy arrangements: "Jingle Bells," "Deck the Halls," "Joy to the World," "Silent Night," "Away in a Manger," "Hark! The Herald Angels Sing," 14 more. Illustrations. 48pp. 8¼ x 11. 0-486-29718-7

NURSERY RHYMES AND NURSERY SONGS, J. W. Elliott. Classic collection of nursery rhymes set to music was, for decades, one of the most beloved of children's songbooks. J. W. Elliott's melodies perfectly capture the charms of these verses; many, including "Sing a Song of Sixpence," have become inseparable from the original rhymes. Lavishly illustrated with 66 beautiful engravings by the Dalziel brothers—renowned Victorian-era illustrators of children's books. 128pp. 8⅜ x 11. 0-486-43806-6

ONE HUNDRED ENGLISH FOLKSONGS, Cecil J. Sharp (ed.). Border ballads, folksongs, collected from all over Great Britain. "Lord Bateman," "Henry Martin," "The Green Wedding," many others. Piano. 235pp. 9 x 12. 0-486-23192-5

"PEG O' MY HEART" AND OTHER FAVORITE SONG HITS, 1912 & 1913, Stanley Appelbaum (ed.). 36 songs by Berlin, Herbert, Handy and others, with complete lyrics, full piano arrangements and original sheet music covers in black and white. 176pp. 9 x 12. 0-486-25998-6

PETRIE'S COMPLETE IRISH MUSIC: 1,582 Traditional Melodies, George Petrie (ed.). The work of 100 years and three generations of archivists, this compilation, which originally appeared in 1905, encompasses the musical wealth of a nation. 448pp. 8⅜ x 11. 0-486-43080-4

POPULAR IRISH SONGS, Florence Leniston (ed.). 37 all-time favorites with vocal and piano arrangements: "My Wild Irish Rose," "Irish Eyes are Smiling," "Last Rose of Summer," "Danny Boy," many more. 160pp. 0-486-26755-5

"A PRETTY GIRL IS LIKE A MELODY" AND OTHER FAVORITE SONG HITS, 1918–1919, David A. Jasen (ed.). "After You've Gone," "How Ya Gonna Keep 'Em Down on the Farm," "I'm Always Chasing Rainbows," "Rock-a-Bye Your Baby" and 36 other Golden Oldies. 176pp. 9 x 12. 0-486-29421-8

A RUSSIAN SONG BOOK, Rose N. Rubin and Michael Stillman (eds.). 25 traditional folk songs, plus 19 popular songs by twentieth-century composers. Full piano arrangements, guitar chords. Lyrics in original Cyrillic, transliteration and English translation. With discography. 112pp. 9 x 12. 0-486-26118-2

"THE ST. LOUIS BLUES" AND OTHER SONG HITS OF 1914, Sandy Marrone (ed.). Full vocal and piano for "By the Beautiful Sea," "Play a Simple Melody," "They Didn't Believe Me,"—21 songs in all. 112pp. 9 x 12. 0-486-26383-5

SEVENTY SCOTTISH SONGS, Helen Hopekirk (ed.). Complete piano and vocals for classics of Scottish song: *Flow Gently, Sweet Afton, Comin' thro' the Rye (Gin a Body Meet a Body), The Campbells are Comin', Robin Adair*, many more. 208pp. 8⅜ x 11. 0-486-27029-7

SONGS OF THE CIVIL WAR, Irwin Silber (ed.). Piano, vocal, guitar chords for 125 songs including "Battle Cry of Freedom," "Marching Through Georgia," "Dixie," "Oh, I'm a Good Old Rebel," "The Drummer Boy of Shiloh," many more. 400pp. 8⅜ x 11. 0-486-28438-7

STEPHEN FOSTER SONG BOOK, Stephen Foster. 40 favorites: "Beautiful Dreamer," "Camptown Races," "Jeanie with the Light Brown Hair," "My Old Kentucky Home," etc. 224pp. 9 x 12. 0-486-23048-1

35 SONG HITS BY GREAT BLACK SONGWRITERS: Bert Williams, Eubie Blake, Ernest Hogan and Others, David A. Jasen (ed.). Ballads, show tunes, other early 20th-century works by black songwriters include "Some of These Days," "A Good Man Is Hard to Find," "I'm Just Wild About Harry," "Love Will Find a Way," 31 other classics. Reprinted from rare sheet music, original covers. 160pp. 9 x 12. (Available in U.S. only) 0-486-40416-1

*Available from your music dealer or write for **free** Music Catalog to*
Dover Publications, Inc., Dept. MUBI, 31 East 2nd Street, Mineola, NY 11501
*Visit us online at **www.doverpublications.com***